Lakewood Memorial Library

IN MEMORY OF

Mr. and Mrs. William
Wigley, Jr.

PRESENTED BY

Alfred A. McCray
Jane Wigley McCray
SWCS Class of 1950

Be a Zillionaire

The Young Zillionaire's Guide to Investment and Savings

Meg Green

rosen
central

I'd like to dedicate this book to my husband, Todd Dawson, who believes in my dreams; my parents, Nate and Margie Green, who taught me to follow my dreams; and my favorite banker, Aunt Ann Fitzgerald, who knows how to save money to make dreams come true.

Published in 2000 by The Rosen Publishing Group, Inc.
29 East 21st Street, New York, NY 10010

Library of Congress Cataloging-in-Publication Data

Green, Meg
    The young zillionaire's guide to investment and savings / Meg Green.
      p. cm. — (Be a zillionaire)
    Includes bibliographical references and index.
    Summary: Explains the basic economic principles of investing and savings.
    ISBN 0-8239-3261-3
    1. Investments—Juvenile literature. 2. Savings and investment—Juvenile literature.
[1. Investments. 2. Savings and investment.] I. Title: Guide to investments and savings. II. Title III. Series.
HG4521 .G695 2000
332.6—dc21   00-25496

TABLE OF CONTENTS

Who Wants to Be a Zillionaire?

So you want to be a zillionaire? You want to have so much money that you can hire Bill Gates to count it. You want to be free to buy anything you want, go anywhere you want, and do anything you want. Hello, lifetime supply of ice cream! Check out my new cable channel, MeTV! What do you think of my new car? So I can't drive yet, here's my chauffeur!

Put those spending dreams on hold because the secret to becoming a zillionaire is not spending. It's saving.

How do you think most people get to be zillionaires anyway? Did they win the lottery or a television quiz show? Work as a professional athlete or a movie star? Inherit money from a rich relative?

You may be surprised to learn that most millionaires did none of that. They got rich by saving and investing their money, one dime at a time, one dollar at a time. About 80 percent of millionaires are self-made.

Surprised? Many adults would be, too. In a recent survey, 27 percent of adults said their best chance to get half a million dollars or more in their lifetime was by winning a lottery. Wrong! The reality is you're more likely to get hit by lightning than to win the lottery.

If you want to become a zillionaire, your best bet is to save and invest your money.

Can you become a zillionaire? Sure, says Selena Maranjian, a financial advisor who writes for The Motley Fool, an on-line site that teaches people how to invest.

"Kids are almost guaranteed to become millionaires if they regularly save and invest a small amount of money," Maranjian says. "They can definitely become millionaires. The more you can learn about it, the better, and the earlier you start, the better. If you start saving and investing when you are fifteen, by the time you're sixty-five you'll have an amazing amount of money."

Consider this: If you invested $50 a week and received 9 percent interest, you'd have $1 million in forty years. That's a lot of ice cream.

What Is Investing?

Investing is using money like a magnet to attract more money. Have you ever heard that money doesn't grow on trees? It doesn't, but it can be used as a seed to grow more money.

The money that your seed money earns is called interest, or return. Some investments, like a bank, promise to give you your seed money back, plus interest, at the end of a period of time. Other investments, like some stocks, offer no guarantees that you'll get your seed money back at all. You must be crazy to risk losing your seed money, right?

That's where investing gets tricky. While it may sound crazy to put your seed money at risk, by doing so, you could earn a higher return and your money could grow faster. You have to learn about risk and decide what kind of risk you are willing to take.

The good news is, some investments get less risky the longer you hang on to them. And as a teen, that's one thing you've got going for you: time.

Usually, the safer the investment, the lower the return, and the riskier the investment, the higher the return. Because of this, some investments are better for short-term savings, such as putting aside money to buy a bike or a video game later this year. You don't want to lose your seed money, or principal, if you have plans for it in the near future.

On the flip side, some investments are better for long-term goals, such as paying for college or starting a business, because over a longer period of time, the risk of you losing your money lessens.

This book will help you sort out the different types of investments and ways of investing, and also show you how to find money to invest.

You Need a Plan!

It can take years of saving and investing to become a zillionaire, but the earlier you start, the sooner you'll reach your goal.

The one thing that millionaires have in common is they watch how they spend their money. They decide what is more important: something they want today or something they may need tomorrow. To do this, they budget their money, or plan how they will spend or save their money.

To start getting rich, you have to start saving money. Every penny counts. Most kids get money through gifts, allowances, and jobs. No matter how you get your money, you can start to make a plan for using it.

Mmmm, Money Pie!

Think of your money like a pie, and cut your pieces carefully.

Some financial advisors recommend saving about one-third of your money for long-term goals, like buying a car or going to college. Another third of the money should be saved for short-term goals, like buying a bike or a new sweater. For the remaining third, some people like to set aside a percentage for charity and the rest for small expenses. If that plan is too strict for you, consider putting aside just 10 percent of your money for saving and investing.

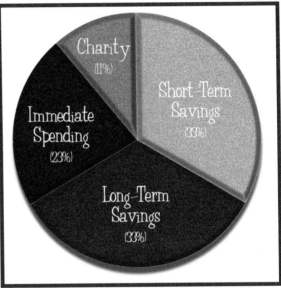

Make a Goal

Don't think of budgeting as going on a financial diet, but as setting aside a couple pieces of pie for later. It might help to think about your ultimate goal, whether it's going to college or buying a video game. And remember, the money you set aside could grow to give you a larger piece of that pie tomorrow!

"The key thing to remember is, saving is a habit," says Irene Leech, a professor of consumer studies at Virginia Tech, and consumer education specialist with the Virginia Cooperative Extension. "It's something everyone, kids and adults, needs to work on."

Save $5 a week and you would have $260 saved in a year, $1,300 in five years, and $2,600 in ten years. However, if you saved that money and invested it at 6 percent interest that's compounded, or added, quarterly (or four times a year), you would get $266 in a year, $1,503 in five years, and $3,527 in ten years.

Jayne Pearl, author of the book *Kids and Money*, says the key is to have a goal. "I don't know any adult who saves just for the heck of it, and kids shouldn't be expected to, either," Pearl says. She says teens may want to save for things such as a car, computer, or college.

If it's smart to save money, it's also smart to spend your money wisely.

Some teens have a "cooling off" period and won't purchase anything over $30 to $50 without taking at least twenty-four hours to think about it. That helps them avoid impulsively buying something they don't really want or need.

Be Cheap

Instead of spending $40 on a new pair of blue jeans at a department store, you could buy a used pair from a thrift store for $10. Instead of spending $5 to eat lunch out, bring a sandwich from home. Instead of spending $8 to go to a movie, you could see it at a matinee or wait until it's on video.

When you decide there is something you really do want to buy, shop around to find the best price. Something in one store may be cheaper in a different store.

There's nothing wrong with spending money to do

the things you really want to do, whether it's pay full price for a new sweatshirt or see a movie opening night. But you should be making a conscious decision to spend your money that way, not just letting it slip through your fingers. You don't want to wake up with an empty wallet and think, "Hey, where did all my money go?"

Write It Down

Speaking of forgetting where your money goes, it's a good idea to write down what you've done with your money. You can use a notebook to write down what money you get and where you put it—whether you invest it in stocks, keep it in your bank account, or spend it on soda. You may keep a separate journal to keep track of individual investments. Or you could save your receipts in envelopes, one for every month.

Keeping records of how you spend your money is very important and is a skill you will use the rest of your life. Sloppy bookkeeping can cost you money. In the future, if you lose a bill and don't pay it on time, you may face penalties. You can't touch some investments until a certain period of time has passed or you will get fined, so it's important to know how much money you need for everyday things.

Writing down where your money goes is also a good way for you to see how you are spending your money. Did you know that spending 65 cents to buy a soda every day means you're spending $237.25 a year on sugar and

water? Maybe you'd rather spend that money on a new snowboard or put it toward paying for college.

Now that you are ready to save money, let's talk about how you can invest it and let it grow for you!

Keep a record of how you spend your money.

Become Your Money's Boss

P. T. Barnum

"Money is a terrible master, but an excellent servant," said P. T. Barnum, circus legend.

Saving money is great because that's building a pile of money. (And who doesn't want a pile of money?) But investing is putting your money to work for you to make more money. It's turning your money into your servant.

When you invest money, you can earn interest.

To calculate interest, you multiply the dollar amount by the percentage of interest. For instance, to find the interest earned on a one-time investment of $100 invested at an annual rate of 5 percent, you would multiply the $100 by 5 percent, or 0.05. That would be $5 in interest earned your first year, or $105.

Just as a magnet grows more powerful as it gets bigger, the bigger your money pile gets, the harder it can work for you and the faster it can grow by attracting more money. That's the magic of compound interest, which is the return that your interest earns.

To compound the interest, you calculate future interest based on your principal and what return your principal has earned so far. So in the second year

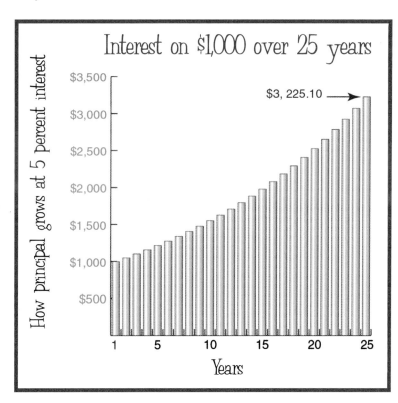

Interest on $1,000 over 25 years

$3, 225.10

How principal grows at 5 percent interest

$3,500
$3,000
$2,500
$2,000
$1,500
$1,000
$500

1   5   10   15   20   25

Years

of your investment in the above example, you would calculate the interest based on $105. Multiply $105 by 5 percent and you earn $5.25 in interest. Add that to your $105, and now you have $110.25 at the end of your second year. In the third year, you'd multiply $110.25 by 5 percent to earn $5.51 in interest. Now you have $115.76. See how it works?

If you kept that $100 invested at 5 percent, it would grow to $322.40 in twenty-five years.

Let the Money Grow

Benjamin Franklin said, "Remember, time is money." The longer you keep your investments, the more your money grows.

Here's an example:

 Save $25 a week and invest it at 5 percent, and it will grow to $166,020 over forty years.

 Save $25 a week and invest it at 7 percent, and it will grow to $286,030 over forty years.

 Save $50 a week and invest it at 5 percent, and it will grow to $332,020 over forty years.

 Save $50 a week and invest it at 9 percent, and it will grow to $1,021,910 over forty years. That's a million clams, folks. If you had just tucked that $50 a week into a shoe box, you'd have only $104,000 in forty years.

Inflation Is a Foe

Earning interest can help you fight inflation. Inflation is the word that describes how things get more expensive every year. A few years ago, you could get a soda from a machine for about 45 cents. Now the price is 65 cents or higher, even $1—or more—in some places (like at the beach in July). This means your money doesn't go as far as it used to. Just ask your parents how much a candy bar cost when they were a kid. (Tell them to skip the story about walking six miles to school every day, uphill both ways, with a wood stove strapped to their backs to keep warm.)

Three factors determine how investments grow: how big the principal is, how much time it has to grow, and what interest rate it grows at.

Because time is a major factor in how investments grow, the earlier you start saving and investing, the better. If you waited until you were thirty-five to invest $100, it could grow to $9,540 by the time you turned sixty if you invested it at a 20 percent rate of return. But if you invested $100 when you were fifteen at that same rate, by the time you were sixty you'd have $365,726.

Even if your investment had a lower rate of return, say 10 percent, if you invested that $100 at thirty-five you'd have $1,083 when you were sixty, twenty-five years later. But if you invested $100 when you were fifteen at 10 percent, you'd have $7,289 when you turned sixty.

72 Is Cool

One more thing about interest . . . check out the cool rule of 72. Divide 72 by the interest rate you are earning, and the number you get is how many years it will take to double your investment. At an interest rate of 6 percent, take 72 and divide it by 6, and your money would double in twelve years. If you found a higher interest rate to invest at, say 12 percent, you would double your money in six years.

So, now that you are interested in interest, let's find out how to earn some.

Remember, time is money.

The Many Roads of Investing

To earn interest, you have to let someone else have your seed money, or principal, for a while. That's investing. And all investing comes with a certain amount of risk, so it's important to understand what that risk is.

There are seven basic types of investments: banks, stocks, bonds, mutual funds, real estate, commodities, and collectibles. Some are riskier than others, and some are easier than others for kids to invest in. For some investments, you may need the help or permission of a parent or adult if you're younger than eighteen. Let's just run down what the different investments are, and discuss them in more depth a little later.

Banks

Banks, credit unions, and savings and loans provide the most basic way of saving and investing. They are all private institutions where you can keep your money. They differ in who runs them and who regulates them, but mostly they offer the same types of saving and investing possibilities.

Banks are in business to make money and are owned by private companies. Credit unions are owned by their members, who pool their money together to offer loans to each other. Savings and loans can be owned by either a private company or an association of members.

Your money is safe in a bank because it's protected by insurance. Most banks are protected by the Federal Deposit Insurance Corporation, while credit unions are protected by the National Credit Union Share Insurance Fund. If the bank or credit union goes bankrupt or out of

Banks pay you interest for letting them keep your money.

business, the U.S. government will make sure you get your money back, up to $100,000. Some savings and loans are not required to have deposit insurance, but most do anyway because no one would want to put their money there if they didn't feel it would be safe. If you, or your parents, choose a savings and loan, ask them if your deposit is protected by insurance.

For now, let's call them all banks.

While the banks have your money, they use it to make loans to other people. They pay you interest for letting them keep your money for a while, then they make loans to other people at a higher interest rate, so they get paid back more money than they lend over time. This is one way they make a profit. In return for the money you've loaned them, they give you a piece of the action, but a pretty small piece. That means the interest rate they pay you is usually fairly low and may not even be higher than the rate of inflation.

Stocks

Buying stock means becoming part-owner of a company. Stockholders, also called shareholders, share in the company's success or failure. If the company makes money, you will share in its profit. If the company loses money, you will share in its losses. As a shareholder, you can vote on certain things that the company wants to do. The number of votes you have is based on the number of shares of stock you have. Stocks change in price as they are bought and sold on the stock market, which is a type of auction.

Historically, the stock market has the best rate of return of any investment in the long term. In the short term, however, stock prices rise and fall every day, so stocks should be considered a long-term investment.

Bonds

Bonds are another way companies and governments raise money. Bonds are a type of loan, except instead of going to the bank to get it, companies and governments go to private investors. Treasury bills, called T-bills, are short-term loans to the government (for periods less than a year). Treasury bonds, called T-bonds, are long-term loans to the federal government (ten years or more). If the government needs to raise $10 million to build a new school, it can divide that $10 million into 1,000 bonds worth $10,000 each (or 10,000 bonds worth $1,000 each). People who buy the bonds are guaranteed a certain return at the end of a set time period, say ten years. Over that ten-year period, the bondholders receive interest payments, just like they do from a bank.

The downside of bonds is if you sell yours before the ten-year period is up, you may face penalties, which will cost money. Also, some bonds are riskier than others, which is something to be aware of. Except for U.S. savings bonds, most bonds require a high deposit and aren't very easy for kids to invest in directly.

Mutual Funds

Mutual funds are a team of individual investors who pool their money together to buy a collection of stocks or bonds. A mutual fund company has a professional manager who picks which companies to invest in or which bonds to buy. As an investor, you buy a piece of the mutual fund, and you share in the profits or losses of the fund as a whole. It's an easy way to invest because someone else worries full-time about which companies might be profitable and which may lose money. In a mutual fund, you don't have as much control over your individual investment and might not even know what companies the mutual fund owns stock in. They also may require a high initial investment.

You can research mutual funds on-line in several places, including www.morningstar.com and www.fundspot.com.

Real Estate

Investing in real estate, such as land or buildings, is difficult for kids because of the size of the investment that is usually required. It means buying a building or property today for a lot of cash, and hoping that you can sell it later for more money than you paid for it.

For many Americans, their biggest single invest-ment is their home. Most people borrow money and get a loan—called a mortgage—to buy their house, and as they pay off the loan, they earn equity. Equity is the value of their assets, or money, minus their debt, or what they still owe on the mortgage.

A lot of people buy property by getting a loan, which is extremely difficult for teens to do. However, if you are interested in investing in real estate, you can consider a Real Estate Investment Trust, or REIT. REITs work like mutual funds but invest in many different properties instead of buying stock in many different companies.

Commodities

Commodities refer to products, such as corn, soybeans, gold, silver, or oil. At commodity exchanges, instead of buying and selling stocks, which are part-ownerships of companies, traders buy and sell contracts. The contracts are legal agree-ments to buy or sell commodities, such as wheat, at a future date. The hope is that when that day comes you'll be able to sell your wheat for more than you agreed to pay for it today.

It's a bit complicated and difficult for kids to invest in commodities. If you are interested, though, take a look at the Chicago Mercantile Exchange at http://www.cme.com or the Chicago Board of Trade at http://www.cbot.com.

Collectibles

Collectibles, like Beanie Babies, Star Wars toys, and baseball cards, may seem like a fun way to invest. Something you got for $3 today might be worth $300 tomorrow. And you may feel safer being able to actually touch your investment, unlike the money you put into a bank, stocks, or a mutual fund.

Buying collectibles may seem like fun, but it may not be the best way to invest your money.

But collectibles may not be the best way to invest your money. It's difficult to know what kind of collectibles will be valuable ten, twenty, or thirty years from now. Plus, for many collectibles to be valuable in the future, they must be in mint, or unused, condition. And what fun is a toy if you can't play with it?

That's a quick look at different ways to invest your money. So what should you do first?

23

Bank On It!

Now let's talk about short-term, low-risk investments, which is where you want to put your money for things like buying in-line skates or a compact disc player later this year.

Most financial advisors will tell you that the place to go for safe, short-term saving is a bank. There are several different places you can put your money in the bank; most will require permission from a parent or guardian.

Savings Account

A savings account is like your own personal piggy bank, except you keep it at the bank, where it is safe from robbers—including brothers and sisters—and earns some interest.

After filling out some paperwork at the bank, you'll get either a passbook savings account or a regular savings account. Both come with little ledger books to keep track of what money you put into the bank, what you take out, and what interest you earn.

With a passbook savings account, you bring the book to the bank every time you are depositing, or putting money into the account, and every time you withdraw, or take money from the account. The teller—that's the person behind the counter at the bank—keeps track of your deposits and withdrawals by marking your passbook.

With a regular savings account, it's up to you to keep track of your deposits and withdrawals. You'll have to fill out a little slip of paper every time you make a deposit or withdrawal, and update your ledger book yourself. The bank will also keep a record. With either a passbook or regular savings account, you'll get a printout, or statement, from the bank every month or every quarter. The statement will show you your balance, or how much is in your account, plus any deposits, withdrawals, or interest earned in that time period.

Savings accounts are pretty simple, and

you can withdraw money anytime you like. Shop around and talk to a few banks to find the highest interest rate you can.

Money Market Funds

A money market fund works sort of like a savings account, only the bank is investing the money in short-term investments, like bonds, to make its money. It's actually a form of mutual fund. In a money market, your money may earn a higher interest rate than in a standard savings account, but a money market account may have more restrictions. Some banks require a minimum deposit before you can open a money market account, and some limit how many times a month or year you can withdraw money from the account.

Certificates of Deposit

A certificate of deposit, or CD, is similar to a money market fund. Banks also usually require you to deposit a minimum amount in a certificate of deposit. But a CD, may have even more restrictions on when you can take your money out.

A certificate of deposit is a safe place to invest money that you wont need for a while.

In return for interest, you agree to keep your money in the CD for a certain length of time—from three months to three years. It's a safe place to set aside money that you know you won't need for a while.

U.S. Savings Bonds

The federal government raises money by selling U.S. savings bonds, which you can also buy at the bank or even on-line. By buying a bond, you are loaning your money to the United States government for a certain period of time. In return, when you cash the bond, you earn interest.

Build a Strong Foundation First

Investing is like a ladder. You want to establish a solid, low-risk base for your money before you reach for higher, riskier investments. The above investments are a good place for a new investor to start, and you will always want to keep some of your money in these safe places. But once you have established your investing and saving foundation, you may want to consider taking on investments with greater risk—and greater rewards.

Let's now take a look at some ways to earn a higher level of interest, which will make your investments grow faster.

Stock It to Me!

"Stocks are the best investments for anyone with a longtime horizon to save," Maranjian says.

That's because over time, stocks tend to have a better rate of growing interest. From 1926 to 1997, the stock market has grown by an average of about 11 percent a year. Some stocks have grown even faster.

When McDonald's first sold its stock in 1965, it sold for $22.50 a share. If you had bought ten shares back then, they would have been worth more than $280,000 by December 1998.

Overall, stocks grew faster than Treasury bills and long-term government bonds.

Stocks are not so good for short-term investments, however, because while over time they have

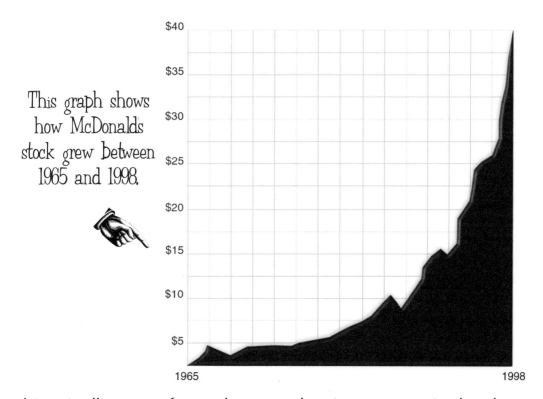

This graph shows how McDonalds stock grew between 1965 and 1998.

historically outperformed every other investment, in the short term, stocks can be a roller coaster ride that goes down as well as up. In 1987, the stock market fell almost 23 percent in a single day. That means people lost, not gained, money, and could have lost part of their principal investment.

Some Basics About Stocks

Price
Stocks range in price from less than $1 to thousands of dollars. Berkshire Hathaway, the parent company of Geico Auto Insurance and Dairy Queen, has stock that cost as much as $81,000 a share in 1999.

Companies raise money by selling stock. The stock price is based on lots of different things, including how the company is doing and whether people want to buy the stock.

In the biggest stock exchange, the New York Stock Exchange, traders buy and sell shares of stock in a giant auction. The price of stocks constantly changes, depending on how many people want to buy a specific stock compared to how many people want to sell it. This is the basic economic rule of supply and demand. If the supply is greater than the demand, the price falls. If the demand is greater than the supply, then there's not

The New York Stock Exchange

enough stock to go around and the price goes up. Once you have bought your stock, you want the price to go up. That means your share is worth more than you paid for it, and if you sold it, you'd make a profit.

Symbols

Traders use a method of shorthand, also called a ticker symbol, to identify a company. For instance, the symbol for McDonald's is MCD, and the symbol for Coca-Cola is KO. To find out what a company's symbol is, you can look it up on several Web sites, such as http://finance.yahoo.com or www.justquotes.com.

Dollars And Cents

Until recently traders thought in terms of dollars but not cents. Instead of using pennies, they break dollars into eighths and sixteenths. An eighth of a dollar is 12.5 cents and a sixteenth of a dollar is 6.25 cents. A stock could sell for $1 1/16, or $1.0625. As of July 2000, the stock market began to record transactions in dollars and cents, which is much easier to understand.

Dividends

When a company is profitable, the people who run the company may decide to share some of the profits with stockholders by issuing dividends. A dividend is a share of the company's profits that the company sends to its shareholders. Some companies allow you to use dividends to purchase additional shares of stock. This is called a dividend reinvestment program, or DRIP.

Splits

When a company's stock reaches a certain price, the company's board of directors can also decide to split the stock.

This can mean that instead of owning a single share worth $50, if the stock splits you could own two shares of stock each worth $25. That keeps the stock affordable.

Over time, stock splits can add up.

In 1919, one share of Coca-Cola sold for $40. If someone in your family bought one share of that stock then, with stock splits and by reinvesting their dividends, they'd have 99,616 shares worth $6.6 million in 1998.

How Can You Tell Which Stock to Buy?

Some financial investors will tell you to invest in products or companies you know or like. That's because buying a stock means becoming a part-owner in a company. If you are going to be a part-owner, make sure you like the company.

How Do You Pick a Winning Stock?

There is no guaranteed, sure-fire way to tell if a stock will make money or lose money because no one knows what will happen in the future.

There are thousands of ways to pick a company to invest in, but generally, you should look at the company and judge how successful you think it will be. You can review a company's annual report, which is sort of an update on how the company performed in the last year. You can talk to other investors, parents, teachers, and friends to see what they think.

So How Do You Go about Buying Stock?

For starters, if you're under eighteen, you may need some help from a parent or another adult. Parents can act as custodians for their children's stock under the Uniform Transfers to Minors Act. Here are some ways to buy stock:

 Go through a broker, who is a professional that sells stocks. This can be expensive because most brokers charge a set fee whether you buy one share or 100. A lot of brokers may not want to sell you just a single share. If your parents or another adult who is close to you buys stock this way, you can ask them to tack on a share or two to one of their orders. A parent can also open a joint brokerage account that he or she can control until the child turns eighteen.

 Join or start an investment club. Some schools have programs where kids can invest a small amount of money monthly. If your school doesn't have one, you can buy a youth membership with the National Association of Investors Corporation, a nonprofit organization dedicated to teaching people how to invest. The NAIC has a youth investment club; for more information, call them at (877) 275-6242.

 Some companies will let you buy stock directly from them, either with an initial purchase or through a dividend reinvestment program. Some companies may require an initial investment of $250 or more, or require you to already own at least one share of stock.

The Feeling Is Mutual

While you are learning which individual companies you want to buy stock in, you can consider buying into a mutual fund. Again, most states require that parents set up mutual fund accounts as a custodian if children are younger than the minimum age, which ranges from eighteen to twenty-two, depending on the state.

Like a shareholder owning part of a company, a shareholder in a mutual fund owns part of a pool of money. The mutual fund company uses the pool of money to buy stock and bonds in other companies, and shareholders share in the mutual fund's successes and failures.

A mutual fund's past performance is no guarantee of future performances. For example, just because the mutual fund boasted a 25 percent growth last year, that doesn't mean it won't trip up and lose money this year. As with any high-risk investment, you have the potential to earn a higher return than with a low-risk investment, such as a bank investment.

Spread Out

Mutual funds allow kids to diversify, or spread out, their investments in a way they probably couldn't do by buying individual stocks. It's important to not carry all of your eggs in one basket because if something happens to that single basket, you'll lose your entire nest egg. Because mutual funds invest in so many diverse companies, if one single company does poorly it may not hurt the mutual fund overall.

Most funds require a minimum investment of $1,000 or more. Some newer mutual funds now cater to kids and invest in companies that kids know and like.

Many Types of Funds

Mutual funds come in many different breeds, and there are thousands of individual ones to choose from. Large-cap funds invest in the 250 largest companies in the country. Midcap funds invest in the next 750 largest companies. Small-cap funds invest in smaller companies.

Some funds are more aggressive, or risky, than others. But remember, with risk comes the potential for higher returns—or greater losses.

In a growth fund, the fund's manager invests in companies that are rapidly growing. In a value fund, the manager invests in companies he or she believes are strong but may have underpriced stock. A blend fund uses a combination of these two philosophies.

There are also funds that invest in international companies, and socially responsible funds, which don't invest in companies that can harm the environment or people.

Mutual funds sometimes have "loads," or fees they charge an investor just to sign on. Look for a no-load mutual fund, although even these will have some fees to pay for the operation of the mutual fund.

When buying into a mutual fund, you should also look at its expenses ratio, which is the proportion of assets that go toward paying for the administration of the fund.

The average mutual fund earns about 2 percent less per year than the stock market performs in general, according to the Motley Fool Web site. Mutual funds also earn less than the market because of the fees shareholders can be charged.

Like stocks, there are thousands of mutual funds you can invest in, and you could spend a lifetime researching which are the best ones. Again, there's no 100 percent accurate way to pick a mutual fund that will be a winner because no one knows what the future holds.

Potential Pitfalls (and How to Avoid Them)

8

In the game of Monopoly, if you land on the wrong square, you can end up losing a turn or money. Sometimes bad luck, or the roll of the dice, sends you directly to jail, do not pass go, do not collect $200.

In real life, with real money, bad luck can also hurt you, and there are no get-out-of-jail-free cards. But there are some things you can watch out for to protect yourself.

Checking Accounts

A checking account is like a savings account, a place where you can put your money at the bank. But most checking accounts are not great places for saving money because most banks don't offer interest on checking accounts and many banks may actually charge you a fee to have a checking account. That's because checking accounts are about spending, not saving, money.

Instead of going to the bank to make withdrawals, you can move money directly out of a checking account to another person or business by writing a check, which is a paper I.O.U. In most places, a check is the same as cold, hard cash.

After you write a check or deposit money in your account, you add or subtract the amount from your balance, which is the amount of money you had in the account to start with. Balancing your account is very important because even if you have no money in your account, you can still write checks to people.

When you write a check for more money than you have, the bank will not honor it. A bad check is called a bounced check because the bank will not pay for it and it bounces back to you. This is not good. The person or business to which you wrote the check will be mad and charge you an additional fee for writing the bad check. The bank will also punish you by charging a fee.

Writing bad checks can hurt your credit record, which is what companies look at before deciding if you can have a credit card, car loan, or house loan. You may not need good credit today, but you will in the future. If you intentionally write bad checks, you can also face criminal charges.

Most kids don't need to write too many checks and may not need a checking account until they are older. It's a good experience to have a checking account, but it's a big responsibility, too.

Debt

Another thing to be aware of is borrowing money. Compound interest works both ways: Sure, you can earn it, but if you borrow money, you also have to pay it.

Some teens have credit cards through their parents, or even on their own. Credit cards are dangerous because it's easy to adopt a "spend today, pay tomorrow" attitude. You should never use a credit card for anything for which you can't afford to pay cash today.

Credit cards can charge hefty interest fees.

Credit cards can charge hefty interest fees, which means you are paying even more than bargained for. People mistakenly believe paying just a small payment every month on a card makes things affordable. Not so. If you carry a $3,000 balance on a credit card with a 19.8 percent interest rate and pay the required minimum balance of 2 percent each month, or $15 (whichever is higher) it would take you thirty-nine years to pay off the loan.

Because it is difficult to earn more interest than you are paying on credit cards, it's a good idea to pay off your credit card debts before you start saving and investing money for the future.

Taxes

The government also raises money through taxes. You probably have already had to pay sales tax, which makes you pay a little more every time you buy something. The government will also tax your income, or the money you earn.

Taxes are based on how much money you earn. The more you earn, the higher percentage you have to pay. Most kids don't make enough to worry about paying taxes yet, but if you are successful in saving and investing, eventually the time will come when you do have to pay.

Also, taxes are taken out of most part-time job paychecks, so be prepared to lose part of your work money right away.

Tax rates can change every year, so be sure to talk to your parents or guardians about how your saving and investing could affect their taxes.

If your parents can claim you as a dependent, and your only source of income is the interest you earned on your investment, you can earn up to $700 tax-free in one year. The taxes on what you earn over $700 would probably be taxed at the lowest rate, 15 percent.

Hidden Fees and Charges

You've heard this a couple of times already, but it's worth repeating: Be on the lookout for hidden fees and charges. Ask the bank if your account has a charge, or if you could be charged for taking money out at any time. Ask the mutual fund how much they will charge you to allow you to participate in the fund. Watch out for credit card companies that will charge you to borrow money.

Get-Rich-Quick Schemes

Anything that sounds too good to be true probably is. Don't invest your money in anything you don't fully understand, and don't ever trust your money to anyone who is not a legitimate business.

Parents

What if your parents don't know much about investing? You have to teach them.

"Be the one who teaches your parents," Pearl says. "It's a great opportunity to invest together." She says parents don't have to be ten steps ahead of their kids. "You can learn together," she says.

Overcoming Obstacles

If all this talk is making you worry, don't fret. Here are a few quick tips:

Comparison Shop

Just as you should spend your money carefully and price check anything you want to buy in a couple different places, you can comparison shop to find the best bank, best mutual fund, and best investment to put your money in.

Diversity

Don't carry your entire nest egg in one basket. It's good to have investments in other places. That helps diversify the risk you are carrying.

Don't Get Overwhelmed

This is a lot of information to digest. If you feel overwhelmed, don't give up and do nothing. Start at the beginning. Make a budget. Start to save. Put

Its a good idea to comparison shop for the best investment.

your money in the bank, and keep studying investments until you feel comfortable enough to begin investing.

"Start small," Pearl says. "Put aside a little every month. Buy a stock or two. Invest in a mutual fund. I don't think it has to be all or nothing."

Patience Is A Virtue

You have the power to become a zillionaire. But it will not happen overnight. You have the most valuable tool of all: time. Be patient, and remember, the earlier you start saving and investing, the quicker your money will grow.

GLOSSARY

bonds   Loans to companies or governments. You receive interest by buying a bond.

certificate of deposit (CD)   A bank investment for a set period of time under a set interest rate.

compound interest   New interest that is earned on the principal and the old interest.

dividend   A small share of profits that a company pays to stockholders.

dividend reinvestment programs (DRIPs)   A program that allows investors to use their dividends to buy additional stock.

inflation   An increase in the amount of money needed to buy things.

interest   What someone pays to borrow money.

principal   Your seed money, the amount of your original investment before interest.

risk   How safe your principal is. Generally, low-risk investments earn low interest, and high-risk investments earn higher interest—but the potential for a big gain can also mean a potential for a big loss.

stock   A portion or share of ownership in a company that is traded publicly.

stock markets   Where stocks are bought and sold, or traded.

For More Information

Organizations

Young Americans Bank & Education Foundation
311 Steele Street
Denver, CO 80206
(303) 321-2265
Web site: http://www.theyoungamericans.org

Free Brochure

6 Steps to Six-Figure Savings: Start Building Your Wealth Today!
Consumer Federation of America
1424 16th Street NW, Suite 604
Washington, DC 20036
(202) 387-6121
Web site: http://www.consumerfed.org

Web Sites

A. G. Edwards & Sons' Big Money Adventure
Web site: http://www.agedwards.com/bma/index.shtml

Investing for Kids (a site designed by kids for kids)
Web site: http://tqd.advanced.org/3096

Motley Fool
http://www.fool.com/teens

For Further Reading

Books

Lee, Dwight R., and Richard B. McKenzie. *The Millionaire Next Door.* Marietta, GA: Longstreet Press, 1996.

Lynch, Peter, and John Rothchild. *Learn to Earn: A Beginner's Guide to the Basics of Investing and Business.* New York: John Wiley & Sons, 1997.

Pearl, Jayne. *Kids and Money.* Princeton, NJ: Bloomberg Press, 1998. See also: http://www.kidsandmoney.com.

Magazines

Kids' Wall Street News
Bimonthly, $19.95 a year
(800) 998-5400

NAIC's Young Money Matters
Published by the National Association of Investors Corporation
Five issues per school year $10; for $20, you can also get a youth membership in the NAIC.
(248) 583-6242

Zillions
$16 per year; published by the nonprofit Consumers Union, which also publishes *Consumer Reports.*
(800) 388-5626

INDEX

About the Author

Meg Green is a writer and journalist living in Easton, Pennsylvania. When not writing about finance, she enjoys writing fiction, playing the flute, making jewelry, and Middle Eastern dancing. She holds a B.A. in English from Ithaca College, Ithaca, New York.

Photo Credits

Cover photos © Artville; pp. 11, 26, 39, 42 by Thaddeus Harden; p. 12 © Archive Photos; pp. 16 and 23 © Artville; p. 18 © Bob Firth; p. 20 © Pictor; p. 25 by Shalhevet Moshe; p. 30 © Michael Paras/International Stock.

Design and Layout

Law Alsobrook